An Elephant Never Regrets

Quirks in Verse for Better or Worse

Linda Ann Nickerson

Gait
House
Press

Cover art: Elephant, 19th Century Dutch illustration. Public
domain.

Internal art: Elephant Profile, vintage illustration. Public
domain.

Published in the United States by Gait House Press.

Printed in the United States of America.

2025

ISBN: 978-1-7371383-5-8

AN ELEPHANT NEVER REGRETS

AN ELEPHANT NEVER REGRETS

AN ELEPHANT NEVER REGRETS

Dedication

An Elephant Never Regrets: Quirks in Verse for Better or Worse is dedicated to my grandchildren. May you carry on the legacy of faith and fun that began many generations ago.

Someday, as you read these words, I hope and pray you'll sort out the honor and the humor. Sometimes they're sort of the same thing. You'll probably come to understand that when you're a bit older.

This book is for you, treasured gifts in my life, because I'll always be in your corner.

AN ELEPHANT NEVER REGRETS

Thoughts on Elephants

"Elephants are quite enough."
Agatha Christie

"Nature's great masterpiece, an elephant – the only harmless great thing."
John Donne

"The elephant is never won by anger; nor must that man who would reclaim a lion take him by the teeth."
John Dryden

"I meant what I said, and I said what I meant. An elephant's faithful one hundred percent."
Dr. Seuss

"Women and elephants never forget."
Dorothy Parker

"Cast your doubts aside, and fly."
Dumbo

AN ELEPHANT NEVER REGRETS

Preface

Folks say that an elephant never forgets. That may be so. But I'd like to think that an elephant never regrets, either.

That's not exactly regrettable. If the elephant doesn't forget and doesn't regret, then maybe he needs not fret or upset either. Hey, we can dream.

That may be a lesson for any of us.

Elephants are a curiosity to be sure. We find them fascinating for the way they look and move and interact with one another. Zoological experts studying elephants frequently describe how these remarkable beasts possess emotional complexity, live in clans and herds with clearly defined social structures, and demonstrate both intelligence and loyalty in their relationships. Indeed, what wonders these bulky behemoths may be!

Much of the time, people can be curiosities too -- maybe even more than the peculiar pachyderms.

That's the stuff of this poetry anthology, titled *An Elephant Never Regrets: Quirks in Verse for Better or Worse*. The verses contained within don't exactly poke fun at pachyderms (at least, not much). Mostly, they point to intriguing, inspiring, entertaining, or just plain puzzling characteristics, attitudes, actions, and experiences involving ourselves and others.

Most of these verses don't have anything to do with elephants ... or do they?

Some of the poems may appear to focus on simpler subjects, but the lines often contain more meaning than one might spot in a first reading.

This collection of poems is intended in good-natured humor. Although some verses are ironic or even sarcastic, the primary purpose of such playfulness is for us to laugh **with** one another – not **at** one another.

Because the best fun is when we can actually laugh at ourselves.

Another aim of these verses is to tell life's stories, be they fragile or funny, disappointing or delightful, melancholy or merry, questioning or just plain quirky.

Our tales tell where we came from and how we have become who we are.

Many of the memories contained in the following pages are my own. Plenty more arose out of interactions, shared times with others, and interesting observations. Others were sparked by popular legends, traditions, or even historic or current events. A few were inspired by culture, both new and old.

All of the stories shared and people described in these poems are fictional, at least in part. Identifying details and descriptions have been changed in any instances based on real people to prevent any pointing of fingers or ruffling of feathers. (How's that for mixing metaphors?)

The point is not to spread rumors, smear characters, drum up drama. or tell tales out of school. Admittedly, a certain measure of catharsis can come from the unpacking of confusing, conflicting, caustic, costly, or merely comical experiences. We often find healing that comes in the sharing (hopefully for both writer and reader), even when the particulars of the stories have been altered for people's privacy purposes.

The telling of tales and expressing of memories, either literally or symbolically, can help us to sort through our memories. In doing so, perhaps we may clarify our own perceptions, identify our progress, and rekindle hope for our prospective pursuits – even while we may chuckle a bit at ourselves.

Maybe that's where the learning begins. And maybe it's not really all about elephants.

AN ELEPHANT NEVER REGRETS

An Elephant
Never Regrets

Quirks in Verse
for Better or Worse

AN ELEPHANT NEVER REGRETS

Table of Contents

AN ELEPHANT NEVER REGRETS

Introduction

This collection of poems runs the gamut in every regard without apology.

You might call it a herd of words. And like the elephant, there are no regrets.

Aimed at provoking everything from light chuckles to deep ponderings, the verses contained in this volume intentionally embody miscellany. The subjects, contents, moods, themes, and styles shift dramatically with each turn of a page. Often, that's how poetry works,

Readers may find something for everyone.

Watch for various poetic forms.

This poetry anthology offers an assortment of rhymed and unrhymed poems, along with metered and unmetered varieties.

Readers will find lots of limericks, as that format naturally lends itself to this kind of content.

Plenty of acrostics and rhymed acrostics are included. Such poems contain all-capital-lettered lines, as they represent this tightly structured format with rules for syllables, repetitions, and highlighting.

Rhymed couplets also abound, along with plenty of other rhyming schemes.

Careful readers may spot some visually structured verses and a few poems representing seldom seen styles.

There's also some free verse, if just for good measure.

Poetic language is flexible.

Careful readers may pinpoint some invented and altered words. (Hint/s: Look for "amphibiosity," "'cept," "'gainst," "mem'ry," "sinist'ry ." "sleight-of-hands," "thinked," "'visioned," "wand'ring," and plenty of other examples.) Writers who know the rules of spelling and grammar also know when it's fit to break them on purpose.

Occasionally, modern writers choose archaic words for creative reasons, especially when working within the constraints of rhyme and meter. I've done plenty of that within these pages. Try to find "alas," "ere," "maketh," "thee," "ye," and more. These poems are also peppered with a few shakes of "ain't," "gonna" and "got," which are technically incorrect in proper writing, but have earned acceptance in casual speech.

For whatever it's worth, any product names that made their way into these lines do not imply either critique or endorsement. Those that appear have basically become household words, and they simply fit the subjects and structures of the poems in which they appear.

Tone of voice shifts from poem to poem.

One may employ first-person, while another might use second-person or third-person. None of these aims for actual attribution. A third-person poem might be partially (or mostly) autobiographical, while a first-person one may be based on another's experience or out of the blue. That's one of the advantages of creative writing. The writer is free to structure each work to suit imagination's purpose.

Poetic subjects can have countless origins.

People often assume creative verses come directly from the lives, thoughts, dreams, hopes, and hearts of the poets who pen then. That is often, but not always, the case.

A few of these poems bear clear or somewhat hidden allusions to literature, mythology, or diverse familiar works. Often, favorite tales may be altered in these verses for creative reasons or emphases.

Please take these verses with a grain of salt and more than a smidgen of grace. No ill will is intended, even in the most sarcastically sharp of these poems. The point is that we may all find ourselves in some verses and look and laugh and perhaps even learn.

Read behind the lines.

Poetry can be simple. A poem can paint a picture, tell a story, play with words, or make a statement. Often, it does several of these at once.

Readers who take a moment to ponder and contemplate the content will often find additional purposes in a poem. It may contain parallel or deeper meanings than what appears at first glance. And it's worth the extra look.

As with many forms of artistic expression, a poetry anthology may contain elements that seem to confuse or contrast one another. This is not necessarily contradictory or paradoxical. It is simply the stuff of human creativity, as our minds and imaginations explore life from multiple vantages and stages.

AN ELEPHANT NEVER REGRETS

AN ELEPHANT NEVER REGRETS

AN ELEPHANT NEVER REGRETS

An Elephant Never Regrets

Quirks in Verse for Better or Worse

AN ELEPHANT NEVER REGRETS

Aback at a Lack

Alas, at the outset,
    I pause
To issue a disclaimer cause.
These poems may poke
Or aim for to joke,
Most often at my own faux pas.

Some verses may characterize,
And more than a few might surprise.
Dear reader, I warn:
Oft-times I do scorn
Myself more than content implies.

We grow when we look in and bleat,
Observing our own chaff and wheat.
The stories here told
Remove the blindfold
With details in fiction offbeat.

In telling each tale we pretend
To see from beginning to end.
But mostly we peek

With eyesight oblique,
Assuming we full comprehend.

For all of us face days in flux,
Intent on our own sweet constructs.
If stanzas may point,
Be not out of joint
O'er snapshots of life. That's the crux.

Like elephants marching along,
Each tuning his steps to a song,
We chuckle and stomp –
Rehearsing our romp.
Assuming the right from the wrong.

Just maybe that's how we grow strong.

Abandon Flip

Abandon hope, ye freshly fooled,
By myst'ry numbed and ridiculed.
Before the dawn was yet delayed,
The hand was dealt.
    The game was played.
Alas, by scorn you have been schooled.

Although you may have been misled,
Refresh yourself with truth instead.
Sad lemons pucker,
    yet bring cheer,
Restoring balance,
    hope sincere.
It isn't always in your head.

Though halting feelings flicker by
To banish each elated cry,
Within the heart,
    joy may deploy.
An April Fool may hear,
    "Good boy."
The day is young yet. Fortify!

The burro rests.
    The wine is poured.
The bread is broken,
    weapons stored.
Abandoned hope refills the fool.
Tomorrow is a lot less cruel.
Endurance is its own reward.

Abducted

Alas, I waited,

Breath still bated,

Death feared, hated,

Until that day.

Captured my heart,

Tied it with art,

Every part

Delivered to stay.

About Face

Attachments add
Bare beauty's fad.
Our visage views
Unmask our blues
To truth unclad.

Facades may fall
At altar's call.
Come clean, my soul –
Erased, be whole.

All Talk and No Trousers

Committee meetings,
    sure to stress –
Of old, we'd plan,
     dress for success.
The era's new,
    but not our clothes.
We sign in sloppy,
    waist to toes.
In tie and jacket,
    fancy blouse,
We phone it in from house to house.

And none the wiser,
    we attend;
When life is virtual,
    rules bend.
Technology advances.
    Wowzers!
Now we're all just talk, no trousers.

Apple a Day

Apprehended by a bite,

Prisoners of appetite –

Pulling on a piece of fruit,

Losing ground – full, absolute.

Evermore to face the fright.

Ah, but wait. It's not too late.

Death's no worry at its core.

All along, Creator's door

Ye has beckoned. Come explore.

Amused or Confused

This fabler with reason remote
Was weird as a three-dollar note.
Her spirit would swell;
The stories she'd tell –
With questions too quirky to quote.

Each audience summoned her muse
In cautious but curious cues.
She'd rave, and she'd rant
And somehow enchant,
Pretending to pay all her dues.

They knew they should stop and steer clear,
For sinist'ry still can endear.
Beware, they were warned.
Oh, no, then they scorned,
And yet to her stories gave ear.

A-Sailed

They won a prize, a special cruise.
"Hooray!" they cried. "How can we lose?"
They danced along the entry ramp,
Like two young kids, attending camp.

The noon-day meal was simply great.
She went back for a second plate
Of Caesar salad, lobster claws,
And then they headed for the spas.

Mid-afternoon, the call came out:
"The Lido Deck is serving trout."
They quickly went to find their seats
And stuff themselves with ocean treats.

So, satisfied, they hit the pool,
Where sweet confections made them drool.
A waiter passed umbrella'ed drinks,
As they relaxed and turned bright pink.

By evening, rang out the bell,
And dinner beckoned them, "Oh, swell!"

They donned their fancy garb just then
And headed off to stuff again.

The presentation, it was sweet,
With every fish and fowl and meat.
They skipped the salad bar this time
Because the pastries were sublime.

That night, she hovered on the deck.
A full-blown nauseated wreck.
She stood and wretched over the side;
She'd swallowed everything but pride.

Ass-King for Trouble

Alas,
    an ass did take his ease
To beg the question,
    if you please.
Despite her fears,
She was all ears.
Here end their similarities.

He dared not look her in the eye,
Afraid she'd dreamt
    another guy.
The scene evolved,
And he resolved
To burrow in her heart he'd try.

He wasn't one to drag his feet,
To bide his time
    or be discreet.
This stubborn hack
Did double back;
Took Tania far from Easy Street.

Perhaps she saw right through his tricks,
But methinks she was
    out for kicks.
When dreamers dwell
    'neath spinner's spell,
The wake-up's anything but swell.

Thus, by the Bard
    for which he starred,
The donkey dude defied her guard.
The burro's bray
The lass did sway,
And followed up with disregard.

Betta Bigdeal

My colleague Betta Bigdeal there
Is all that and some chips.
Our group does teeter o'er despair,
As Betta stages scripts.

Her stories swirl the straightest locks,
As tangled words she weaves.
Though guile is simple to outfox,
Her own tales she believes.

She dreams she carries influence
Within her tiny hands.
It's mostly discontinuance;
The world, it understands.

We smile and nod and then proceed.
She doesn't have a clue
That to the exit most stampede
Before they bid adieu.

Poor Betta's motoring full-speed,
No compass, key or map.

The social cues, she will not read,
So stretches fill the gap.

We'll never tell her to her face;
Such conflict we've declined.
Besides, we know it's not our place
To manage humankind.

Big Bang

Their lives grew stable. Days were good.
They found a better neighborhood.
To seek serenity, no qualm,
They added codes and intercom.
Then something sounded … like a bomb.

"Hello, police?" the call was placed.
"It's an emergency. Posthaste!"
The squad arrived to hold the laws –
Found no real danger there because
The threat abated. Nothing strange.
Just living by the rifle range.

Within a week or three or four,
They didn't hear it anymore.
It seems they learned just to ignore
Artillery nearly next door.

Big Hitter

A backstop ornament co-ed
In elementary phys. ed –
She couldn't hit
Or use her mitt,
Unpicked and overlooked instead.

They'd crowd the diamond to play ball,
And every student, one and all,
Who loved the game –
No fear of shame –
Awaited captain's welcome call.

At last, the choices would be made:
One player left; didn't make the grade.
The scrawny brain
Would face disdain,
As gym coach would insist she played.

Each turn at bat, she never ran,
For sadly, every pitch she'd fan.
"Strike three!" they'd yell,
Clear as a bell.

Her confidence was in the can.

She'd trudge to outfield with a frown
And cower, her defenses down.
Athletics class
Would slowly pass,
Till time to leave would come around.

The bell would ring its sweet retort,
And off to desks they would report.
As jocks would strut,
Her feelings cut,
For they of her would oft make sport.

Still, she was smartest of the lot –
A miracle of higher thought.
Disparate marks,
Despite their barks –
One day, she out-surpassed their haught.

Ah, her redemption came at last.
She graduated top of class.
And in her speech,
She did beseech,
As sporty bullies failed to pass.

Today, those field stars, true to style,
Field telemarketers and file.
Their captain, she –
Now boss, you see –
Calls all the shots with winning style.

Bliss & Tell

There's no such thing as bliss and tell.
It's just a story none can sell.
No hook or crook to overlook,
Nor makings of a major book.

So we embellish to the nines
And color far outside the lines.
Serenity does not excite,
But flashy fiction surely might.

A daily drama draws more views,
Let's light the fascination fuse.
Discarding facts to favor tales
Will court more readers, boost ad sales.

With details, scuttlebutt uncouth,
Attention triumphs over truth.
What happened to straightforward news?
It simply failed to lure, amuse.

Boredom Busters

Ring the doctor! Call him stat.
Summon here the bureaucrat.
Must inject excitement now –
Wild-eyed wonder, holy cow.

We have an emergency
Of the highest urgency.
Entertain us. We are bored,
And we will not be ignored.

Weakest comedy abounds –
Silly lines, insipid sounds.
Someone's bending our best ears.
Life is not as it appears.

Boredom busters: take your guard.
Entertainment can be hard.
Exercise your finest wit,
Or we'll throw a hissy fit.

Wand'ring minds may take their leave,
Seeking thrill through make-believe –

Sticky subjects to avoid,
Tricky topics, paranoid.

Jokes grow older; quips grow cold.
Stories fail when over-told.
Call a comic with some class,
Or we'll simply take a pass.

Boredom busters, rescue us!
We have nothing to discuss.
Still, we long for lighter times.
Ennui may be cured by rhymes.

Brash Landing (Taking It on the Chagrin)

A fella might indulge to gloat,
Had he not fumbled,
    missed the boat.
The stormy stars
Hummed higher bars
And reckoned his repute remote.

He dreamt his days till time was spent
Expending past
    his heart's content.
Thus sobered, he
Did disagree
To ne'er evolve by shared consent.

Umbrella up, he stepped aloft.
He caught a draft
    and quickly coughed.
The gate was wide;
He slipped inside
To flip and flop for landing soft.

Then, lo, with chill he stopped to peer.
At once, his glance
    became sincere.
He could not bear
The open air,
Bravado dashed by starkest fear.

Breathing

Breathing

Rhythms

Exercise

Anyone's

Trust.

How

Intensely

Need we

Grasp truth?

Breath-o-Lazer

Spraying stories at a gasp,
Hoarsely howling with a rasp,
As they all their ears do clasp –
Waiting for a breath.

Pregnant pauses none may find,
From his issue unassigned.
He'll unburden full his mind –
Sharing every breath.

Others' thoughts may merit speech,
But the moment's out of reach,
Without words they may beseech –
Underneath their breath.

He'll assume that they agree,
While they nod in misery,
Bearing his soliloquy –
Talking them to death.

Breath of God

Boldly

Roaring

Everywhere

At once,

Transferring

Heaven's

Air

Over all the

Frail, but unforgotten –

God grants

Outstanding

Deliverance.

Broke, Fight Again

Boss yells,
> "Duck! Here comes the slip!"
Reaching for your microchip.
On your way,
> you stop, salute –
Kicked out, given dreaded boot –
Evermore smart as a whip.

Fight in faith,
> and go for broke,
If your slot went up in smoke.
Groan and moan;
> you may have guessed –
Here's no setback, but a test,
Truest talents to provoke.

Any day now, watch and see,

Gauging your prosperity.

As your fists find pockets bare,

In your scramble; don't despair,

Nicer doors will part for thee.

Calling Out Clyde

A pompous conductor named Clyde,
With more than
    a pittance of pride,
Would call,
    "All aboard,"
In tone untoward,
Feigned accent with status implied.

For years,
    Clyde conducted his trade,
Enjoying his striped masquerade,
Till hoofbeats rang out
From bandits about,
And left the conductor unpaid.

The crooks bound the sniffy old boy
And left him behind
    like a toy.
There, tied to the stack,
He pondered his lack,
With only himself to employ.

The moral is simple and base:
Our tracks may be
    tricky to trace.
With nose in the air,
Collecting a fare,
Disdain quickly leads to disgrace.

Camel Lots and Trots

His camel has two great big humps.
He sits between them, as he bumps,
A-lumbering 'cross desert sand
In some exotic distant land.

Adventure such does her entrance.
She'd like to try the camel's dance –
To venture forth beyond the fence
And take in sites far past pretense.

Her eyes reality deceive
In stories she can dream, perceive.
The camel jaunt
Her heart may haunt
Within the pages to conceive.

Adventure is her middle name.
Such derring-do she would proclaim.
Put down the book,
And take a look.
It's half-past time to join the game.

Careers and Frontiers

A creative young woman named Ro
Had reached an employment plateau.
She pulled a few strings
To give herself wings,
And now Ro is rolling in dough.

It's not simply seeds that you sow,
Nor how many rows you may hoe.
To aim for the peak,
Though prospects are bleak,
The secret may be whom you know.

Catalogued

Counting chips to make his mark;

An elephant never forgets.

Tally up the deeds done dark,

And he will reclaim your regrets.

Look long beyond the closest past

O'er decades of daily demands.

Guess who can call you to contrast

Untold and unfair sleight-of-hands.

Each mem'ry, tucked in his trunk

Delivers all others to funk.

Cha-Cha-Charlie

There once was a writer named Charlie,
Who'd mastered the art of the parley.
Then somehow by chance,
She started to dance
And turned all the beer back to barley.

Excitement had filled her with glee;
Her readership soared by degree.
So Charlie she rose
On the tips of her toes
And jigged for the rainclouds to flee.

This happy dance caught on like flame,
And Charlie acquired a name.
With shamrocks and plume,
She slid 'cross the room,
So playfully prancing to fame.

Charmed and Dangerous

Prince Smarming was a sneaky sort.
Made every mom a worry wart.
He'd flatter fine,
Use every line,
But truth remained his last resort.

She saw him coming,
    keen to charm
And triggering her creep-alarm.
Too smart to woo,
She saw right through
And met him with a firearm.

He flipped his hair and hit the bricks
To find another, just for kicks.
Each lass he tried
His calls denied –
She'd tipped them off to all his tricks.

Chasing Reverie More Cleverly

Of grief the forethought may be much,
When mortal mercy's out of touch.
If most misgivings do provoke,
We question destiny's cruel joke.

Yet dreams deliver fresh desire;
New expectations we require.
Such tempting visions interest draw,
Provoking earnest yearnings raw.

Then, daring to defy the good,
We struggle far more than we should.
As Tantalus, we might beseech:
Let not our grasp exceed our reach.

Ah, dreams may count for more than sleep,
If faith's full subject do we keep.
And life is only worth a whit
When we our need for Help admit.

Choosing Scrappiness

A woman we knew from our church,
(Don't worry. I shall not besmirch.)
So scrappy and keen,
'Twas nearly obscene,
Her company oft I would search
For answers when left in the lurch.

She wasn't aggressive or rude
Or known for a harsh attitude.
Somehow she held sway
And things went her way,
Perhaps it was her gratitude.
Regardless, she left folks renewed.

Her meekness was mixed with her mirth,
Combined with a smidgen of earth.
She couldn't be crushed
Or, gosh, even hushed,
And bullies would give her wide berth.
We loved her for all that it's worth.

Copping an Excuse?

One Friday evening,
    while driving out West,
Putting her new four-wheel-drive
    to the test,
She spotted the lights,
    which curtailed her fun-fest
And veered for the shoulder then,
    under arrest.

She glanced in the mirror,
    perfecting her smile,
Touched up her bright lipstick
    and smoothed her hairstyle.
She'd talked her way out of this,
    once in a while.
But c'mon, did she think
    she was still juvenile?

"Hey, Ma'am, I just clocked you
    at sixty or more,"
He said, as he leaned on the side
    of her door.

She glanced up and felt
    like a tyrannosaur;
This kid couldn't have been more
    than age twenty-four.

The wee whippersnapper
    was simply polite;
He said not to drive
    like a meteorite.
He wrote a citation
    and bade her goodnight,
Then he hopped in his squad car
    and sped out of sight.

She learned a most difficult lesson
    right there,
For when she was twenty,
    the cops didn't care.
They'd give her a warning
    and say it with flair,
But at sixty, she'd better
    slow down and beware!

Cord Games

Along the rope, each tiny fist
Held to a knot, so none were missed.
Their little feet marched down the hall
From room to room came one and all.

It's no great feat to follow suit
With rules so clear and absolute.
But once we grow and then let go
We scatter off both to and fro.

The ties that bind may wiggle loose,
As we bounce back from trial to truce.
Our hearts may hanker, as we pine
For days we simply held the line.

Core Value

My gym pal Jill does fit the bill.
She operates in her free will.
In any place,
She owns her space,
But never up to overkill.

She shows up strong to hit each rep,
To carve her core and perk her pep.
Here, pushing 60, off she goes,
And where she'll stop, nobody knows.

Could be she's found the youthful fount
And quaffed prodigiously past count.
Explorers' gold
Is oversold,
When vis a vis her spunk's surmount.

Crossing the Lines

Commuting home, I grab my keys
And step inside to take my ease,
When something interrupts me,
    "Geez!"
My stress load rises ten degrees.

    Telemarketer, my friend,
    Test my ring-tone without end.
    Make my cordless ring again,
    And my late dinner hour extend.

What are you hawking with your call?
A raffle for the fireman's ball?
Or garbage bags, our trash to haul?
Gimme a break,
    you know-it-all.

You're raising consciousness for pets?
Collecting funds for army vets?
I've one of each and need no debt.
You're playing telephone roulette.

Telemarketer, my friend,
Test my ring-tone without end.
Make my cordless ring again,
And my late dinner hour extend.

Why can't you just leave us alone?
You make my family grump and groan.
My temper's in the danger zone.
I guess I'll go unplug the phone.

Dip in Denial

A hard-working author named Fink
Once penned a "Dear John" to his shrink.
He ranted and railed.
The missive he mailed,
But wrote with invisible ink.

The doc was confused and perplexed –
Examined the note with no text.
He looked up the fuzz
And gave them a buzz,
Then handed the note and called, "Next?"

Disengaged

Barely twenty, she fell hard.
Oh, her heart, he truly marred.
A looker, always on his guard;
She should have stayed in her own yard.

Her birthday came, and they went out.
Another couple joined the route.
She thought this one would be devout,
And yet she should have carried doubt.

The food was served,
    and plates were cleared,
Just then a tiny gift appeared.
She picked it up;
    inside she peered
And found a ring with gem ensphered.

Her eyes grew large. She didn't believe
So soon she might this gift receive.
She couldn't decide, to stay or leave,
Until her friends began to heave.

The ring was false, and so was he.
The friends convulsed in hearty glee.
Although this prank was played off-key
She sensed relief. She was home free.

They roared with laughter till they cried.
The boyfriend, he was mortified!
Her doubtings then were pacified,
For she would never be his bride.

Dot on the Spot

An underpaid daredevil, Dot,
From cannons afire, she was shot.
Her helmet, she'd clip
For aerial trip,
Until she forgot on the spot.

She climbed in the barrel that night,
Prepared for her usual flight.
The fuse, it was lit;
She cared not a whit,
Not knowing the end was in sight.

The crowds were amazed at the show,
Amused to see angels below.
On heavenly wing,
Dear Dot still may swing.
The ringleader claims it is so.

Duck and Cover

Duck and cover. Here we go.

Underneath the surface, whoa!

Comes a threat we cannot see.

Know now that it comes for thee.

All attend. You may be next.

No silly scam or false pretext.

Decide now not to be perplexed.

Contagious isn't just a threat.

Outrageous how it may upset.

Viral as the story flies

Ear to ear and eyes to eyes.

Rally fast, and empathize.

Dumbed-Down Decision

I'm feeling dumber.
    Ouch! My brain!
The cranium,
    it pounds with pain.
Despite resolve,
    the answers flee
More now than in all history.
That's right.
    It's time to vote again.

The candidates are sounding off.
They stomp and strut
    and scream and scoff.
Perhaps they should return to school,
Revisiting the Golden Rule.
The public needs a stronger quaff.

We harken back to days that fled,
When blood was blue
    and white and red.
Ideals were real
    and stood their ground,

Unfettered by such stupid sound.
I fear the nation's lost its head.

Can we retrace and find the trail
For which our ancestors set sail?
Simplicity may save us yet,
If we can see its silhouette.
May freedom ring and right prevail.

Escaping the Elephant

His bulk, it casts a shadow form
On life that's anything but norm.
His spunk is spent;
The elephant
Has turned his tusks up in a storm.

He stomps his feet
    and flaps his ears
To stimulate the others' fears.
He's half a mind
To act refined.
But look:
    His prey is raising cheers.

"How are you doing?"
    "Fine," they say
And hope we look the other way,
As his charade
There on parade
Outside opinions still may sway.

They beg us not to intercept

Captivity in which they're kept.
His trunk and trust
May be a bust,
As o'er his shadow they have leapt.

Fall A-Board

A tenant was paying his board,
Which seemed more
    than he could afford.
"Why raise it?" he cried.
The landlord just sighed.
"The others moved out,
    'cause you snored."

Fancy Fishing

Poseidon was beside himself.
His heart had knocked him off the shelf.
A mermaid's glance,
With eyes askance,
Reduced the water king to elf.

Amphibiosity desired,
Poseidon with the maid conspired.
He tipped his cup –
Then, swimming up,
The underwater tsar retired.

The moral here is damp, but sure:
Desire dangles danger's lure.

Final Exam? Thank You, Ma'am

How we have missed our intern friend,
As her semester came to end.
She sat beneath a pile of notes:
Equations, glossaries, and quotes.

Then finally,
 the testing stopped,
As bottles waited
 to be popped.
Our sleepless friend
 returned to life,
Thus ending
 academic strife.

With flying colors,
 Kady passed
Her finals,
 from the first to last.
In math and science,
 she excelled,
And every word
 correctly spelled.

She left the others in the dust,
And hurried homeward,
      as she must.
Her loved ones waited,
      holding breath,
And wringing hands like Dame Macbeth.

Our happy scholar shared her news
And quickly banished all her blues.
She's stored her notebooks all away.
Now Kady comes to work for pay.

Flexercising in Utility

I'd pump some iron,
    if I could.
I know that it would do me good.
But oh, so many just desserts
Have set me back.
    My body hurts.

My clothes are snug,
    my form unfirm.
I'm feeling like a pachyderm.
Could make excuses of my years;
Truth is
    my workout's in arrears.

It's time to put aside my fork.
My posture needs a solid torque –
Activity with lots of reps
For abs,
    and arms,
        and quadriceps.

The calisthenics, lifts, and drills,

They throw me into sweats and chills.
How many calories will burn
Before the point of no return?

If I had energy to borrow ...
Guess I'll just exercise tomorrow.

Forsooth-Slayer

A suited bug sprayer, DeVries,
Departed with nary a sneeze.
He set down his gun
And took off, a-run,
Alas, he's allergic to bees.

Because the man sprouted his wings,
Our domicile buzzes and sings.
We hope a deep freeze
Exterminates these
Before we may suffer some stings.

Found in Faith

Along the dial in the void,
Before the dawn has been deployed,
A harried hush may hearken heat
And hold the heart to barely beat.

There marks a moment's murky mist,
Where darkest doubts we may resist –
For finer faith to find us fast,
While wondrous wind wipes off the past.

The Earth may sleep.
    The stars may hold.
What whispers then is to be told.
'Tis only meant for those who wait
For such appointment, half past late.

It changes us to count each chime.
The One we seek is outside Time.

Full of Beans

The coffee bean's a favorite treat
Among the elephant elite.
Recycled through his system grand,
'Twill grace the mug of some gourmand.

Repugnant as the thought may seem,
The epicure calls it a dream.
So bon vivant, Sir Elephant.
Eat all the coffee beans you want.

Stroll the savanna. Take your pick.
Arabica won't make you sick.
What deeper message all this means?
The elephant is full of beans.

Giving Up

They found him underneath his chair.
Who knows how long he languished there.
The tongues wagged wild,
As rumors riled,
With theories flying everywhere.

A chocolate wrapper in his grip
Soon silenced each and every quip.
Disaster fell,
But none could tell:
What caused the strongest one to slip?

He wouldn't plead for help serene.
The poor boy never made a scene.
They missed the point –
Not drink or joint.
He'd simply given up caffeine!

Glossing the Boss

My favorite little sycophant
The party line will ever chant.
He'll bow and scrape
    and then supplant
To climb the ladder,
    yet he can't.

Abundantly unqualified,
His offers, never bona fide –
He keeps the brass much mollified
And offers them his underside.

He caters to the highers-up;
He fetches them the coffee cup.
To them he is a sim'pring pup
Who'll never make the big lineup.

This yes-man, toady, wannabee,
Who kisses up for all to see
Presents no threat to you or me,
Not in the tiniest degree.

Still, he attempts to make his case,
Each time he stoops,
    a shoe to lace.
And though he's in my breathing space,
He'll never rise to take my place.

He's recognized as just a schlock.
His crowings, boastings are a crock.
And as he sits to watch the clock,
His head is on the chopping block.

Got a Grip

The hanger-on, he merits praise.
He perseveres. His dues he pays.
No Easy Street
Will bear his feet,
For in advance he'll cost appraise.

Like strongest forest sapling sure,
Seedling to tree, he stands secure.
No fear of dark
Will raise his bark,
In woods most mossy or obscure.

He won't succumb to jolt or jab.
He'd rather walk than call a cab.
Such efforts earn
Beyond the burn,
For he would rather gain than grab.

And be it ladder, mount, or tree,
This one can climb it handily.
In weather fair
Or foulest air,

He touches not profanity.

Know this: His trust bears sturdy roots
In solid standards, absolutes.
And glory be,
No braggart, he
His self-same horn he never toots.

The tracings of his tresses fall,
To point a pathway for us all.
Though silent still,
He holds on till
The lesser ones find wherewithal.

Guess Who's Peeking Through

Sunshine or moonshine,
A pair of faces appears.
Images deceive.
GUESS WHO'S PEEKING THROUGH.
Images deceive.
A pair of faces appears.
Sunshine or moonshine.

Onlookers decide,
Putting dampers on drollness,
Choosing what to see.
GUESS WHO'S PEEKING THROUGH.
Choosing what to see,
Putting dampers on drollness,
Onlookers decide.

He's Got Mail

A mystery missive arrives with a bill,
Proclaiming a figure that brings on a thrill.
What was his reaction to find it unsealed?
A cynic or gullible,
  what was revealed?

A true sweepstakes winner,
  a sap or a sage?
Was he merely jaded or naïve for age?
As he scans the small print
  to learn of his prize,
We might gauge his odds
  by the look in his eyes.

What wonders await him?
  What fortunes come through?
But wait!
  You and I got the same letter too!

Jibe Ho!

He holds the jib, and I the main;
One gunshot, and we zip.
Look, here we come about again
To heel, careen, and tip.

We clear the marker, turning 'round;
We take the lead and fly
To skim the surf without a sound
Beneath the wispy sky.

My spinnaker, she proudly furls
In yellow, red, and blue
Like many fair beribboned girls
Adorned in every hue.

Again we jibe to catch the wind
O'er shadows in the deep.
What lurks beneath the surface, friend,
Had better be asleep!

Along the homestretch, catch the gust
And watch the sheets respond.

To reach the final mark, we push,
The fleet astern becalmed.

And so the victor's flag we wave;
It flies atop the mast.
And though the others glory crave,
'Tis they who are downcast.

For, lo, the ocean is my love.
The winds have caught my soul.
'Neath cloudy canopies above,
My ship will rock and roll.

Just Joy

I'll here admit it:
    Life is tough.
Some days I think
    I've had enough.
Although I know
    it's all been planned.
It's hard to get the upper hand.

When circumstance goes
    'gainst the grain,
And daily drudgery
    does drain,
I hearken back,
    which takes a choice,
To listen to another voice.

Ridiculous as it may sound,
Truth is, the downcast
    will be crowned.
When wrong's removed
    and right is raised,
I know Who will be ever praised.

Today is hard.
    There is no doubt.
I'm tempted to prolong my pout.
But I will hold my ground,
    prevail.
For happiness to joy does pale.

Keep on Kidding

A gal who seems guileless and sweet
Cavorts every week on the street.
Each Friday at five
Her drive comes alive.
By Mondays,
    she's red as a beet.

She punches out,
    week after week,
Then lets down her locks,
    long and sleek.
Her eyelids she paints,
Then loosens restraints
To practice
    what gossips misspeak.

Her high-collared blouses she stows
To sing karaoke with beaux.
But each Sunday night,
She's back to stage fright.
The secret is nobody knows.

How long may her secret remain,
Her travel in fast and slow lane?
Like two persons split,
She dares not admit.
This maid still would honor maintain.

Kick in the Class

People wonder: What is class?
Is it a race to win, surpass?
To be the highest of the brass?
How have we come to this impasse?

The classiest of all are sure
One need not be a connoisseur,
Nor crow with boastings immature,
For that would show one just a boor.

So what is class? How is it seen?
Why are so many painted green?
Perhaps the trimming's mere smokescreen,
And class is something more serene.

Is there a source to gain this trait,
Or must we settle, second-rate?
For if we self-congratulate,
Our class, it will evaporate.

For class cannot be bought or sold.
It can't be weighed in grams like gold,

Nor measured as a big billfold.
In fact, true class is pride controlled.

The classiest are first to bend,
And last to strut, preen, or pretend.
They seek, o'er all, not to offend,
And anyone can be their friend.

The cream of crop among us know;
They value those above, below.
They understand, from the get-go,
That everything to God we owe.

When people wonder: What is class?
The question, in itself, is crass.
For this is not a course to pass.
Such folks may need kick in the class.

King of the Bungle

I had a boss.
    Let's call him Gil.
His strongest suit was overkill.
This fellow foul
Did bellow, growl –
The underlings would sip the swill.

He'd call me in to script a speech.
We'd practice.
    I'd try not to preach.
But at the mic,
His rage would strike,
And Gil his ethics would impeach.

The audience of moguls, stars,
Would stagger swiftly to their cars
To take a hike,
No deal to strike.
Thus Gil was left without applause.

Ere long, his train went off the track,
This would-be king and crackerjack.

He blew his top
Without a stop.
Poor Gil, he had a heart attack.

Gil survived, but was retired.
In his absence, much required,
Coffee poured;
Morale restored,
And profits rose, as if inspired.

His second was a quiet sort.
He led a solid, simpler court.
The business grew.
Well, gee, who knew
Success would come from cool comport?

Landfill

Who knows what evil lurks inside
The bedroom of my teen?
I venture forward, petrified:
The zone of quarantine.

Beneath the laundry, two cell phones
And papers on the floor,
The Watergate Tapes, Hoffa's bones,
The Missing Link, and more.

"Clean up this mess!" I loudly bleat.
My neighbors turn and stare.
The window's open, shame complete,
I'm glad I didn't swear!

Let It Be Brie

Sometimes a stinky outer crust
Does hide a tenderness and trust
That comes with waiting and with age
To melt its mold and shell assuage –

So foe to favorite may transform;
The coldest hearts can be made warm.
The best of cultures make it so,
Attracting others to their glow.

Live and Bet Liv

My friend Olivia, Gadzooks!
That girl, she cooks, but not the books.
She masters with a Midas hand
Whatever programs she has planned.

We call on Liv for volunteers,
And naysayers become all ears.
For fundraisers she's dear, deluxe,
And everybody brings the bucks.

Her skills are scary; girl's on fire.
We hope she never does retire.

Making Much

Max, of himself he maketh much –
Holds conversations in his clutch.
As those around are too polite
To call him out;
    no end's in sight.

He pours his overflowing cup,
Just like a choir, warming up.
It's "La-la-la"
    and "Me-me-me."
He sings his solo, though off-key.

And to ourselves, we hope alike
That laryngitis him should strike.
(Or someone has to swipe his mic.)

Making Up Time

Rushed for work and out of gas,
With no time for the looking glass,
She snatched her keys and headed out
To face the daily knockabout.

She tossed her briefcase in the trunk
And grabbed a mug and roll to dunk.
She turned the corner at full tilt,
And raced her neighbor out in guilt.

Somehow, she zipped through every light.
Perhaps she'd make it; she just might.
Her hopes were raised then,
    just a smidge,
Until she saw the tollway bridge.

The entry ramp was jammed with cars,
From rattling heaps to sleek Jaguars.
She sat there waiting for her turn
And listened to her stomach churn.

Her dashboard clock was ticking eight,

Just taunting her that she was late.
The boss would gloat and call her out.
Her well-earned raise would be in doubt.

But, living in the here and now,
She'd have to buy some time somehow.
Her coffee drained,
    she glanced around
To spot efficiency newfound.

Her makeup bag was in her lap,
While she sat in the traffic trap.
So, as she rolled the car an inch,
She put her face on in a pinch.

Her lipstick smeared across her chin;
Her eyeliner was crooked, thin.
Just then, the car began to skid;
Mascara smeared across one lid.

She spilled a compact on her skirt
And hit the brakes,
    now on alert.
The car behind her came too fast
And hit her bumper at full blast.

She stopped and shifted into park
And leapt out, gearing up to bark.
The reason for her sudden strife?
The driver was the boss' wife!

They glared and stared, as if to slur,
With both their tempers much astir.
A cop arrived to part the brawl.
"Cosmetic damages, that's all!"

Mammoth Aspirations

He generally is a thug
    to battle nail and tooth,
And though he cannot cut a rug,
    he dances 'round the truth.

He never went to Oxford,
    barely learned the alphabet.
His graduation picture's lifted
    from the internet.

He grabs the gab in discourse,
    unencumbered by the facts,
And compensates with volume
    in the areas he lacks.

His happiness expands threefold
    each time the fur, it flies.
In retrospection, truth be told,
    believes he his own lies.

Upon the backs of others, he is
    everything he thinked,

Although his reputation large
    one day will be extinct.

His words add wrinkles to his ways;
    his recollect is wooly.
And though he shouts above the herd,
    we understand him fully.

(Bet you though I'd say "bully.")

Mammoth or Mastodon?

A mammoth or a mastodon?
The difference is huge.
From girth to bulk and brain to brawn,
They hold no subterfuge.

In cave or crag, to be succinct,
I'd neither like to greet.
Perhaps we're safe; they're both extinct,
Though that be bittersweet.

The darkest dangers may not lurk
In such gigantic form.
'Tis those that creep and sneak that most,
Misguide and misinform.

Fear not, for both were herbivores,
Preferring plants to meat.
Although they traveled on all fours,
They never sought to cheat.

These days, their bones show up in sand,
As experts lay their claim.

We may not ever understand
Their absence: Who's to blame?

Now if our tusks be out of joint,
We shudder at the thought.
It seems we still have missed the point,
And dodged the wrong onslaught.

Mammoths

Mighty mammoths

All extreme –

Monstrous menace,

Mighty, mean.

On the offense,

Try the scene.

Heaven help us

Stand serene.

Mar for the Course

My car was crunching, hit and run,
While we were lunching, just for fun.

We cannot guess who owned offence,
Because we found no evidence.
No video or paint to scratch,
Just punched and bunched the rear-end hatch.

No witnesses, no "Sorry" note.
It's sad to say,
    "That's all she wrote."
The guilty one had gone away,
And I was left to stew and pay.

Deductible and rates to hike.
I think I'd better ride my bike.

Mirth Control

Takes 20 months or more to birth
An elephant upon the earth.
I can't imagine how to wait
For nigh two years to celebrate.

Her trunk is never out of joint,
Though hormones rage and disappoint.
She'll stand and spray and stop to rest,
And never look the least distressed.

I wonder if her humor's sense
Can carry her from hence to whence.
Perhaps she casts aside her care,
When with a friend she'll laughter share.

Never Nimble

I never knew a nimble note,
With painful practices by rote.
I play by ear,
But so sincere,
Not choosing what composers wrote.

For harmony may soon be sought.
It's neither borrowed, loaned, nor bought.
Notes blending sweet
May often meet
When creativity is caught.

Thus, unexpected, life is found
With melodies beyond profound.
I trip and fall,
But after all,
May I the critics all confound.

Nope Opera

Noes
Or nots
Populate
Endless thinking.

Optimists, rise up!
Propel the song,
Enthusing
Reason's
Aims.

Of Mice and Mien

A hunk of cheese a mouse may catch,
Enticing him beyond his match.
Reward's allure
May him assure
To meet the one who'll him dispatch.

A gifted gamer, most intense
With interest in his own two cents
Might toss a chip,
Shoot from the hip,
To banish common sense from thence.

An easy mark with meek mien,
The jackpot seeker goes all-in.
He eyes the prize
With bleary eyes.
The trap is set in danger's den.

Across the table, truth awaits
And watches folly, sans debates.
He holds his peace
With elbow grease,

The mouse to snare with fortune's baits.

Occasionally, treasures rot –
Like rich rewards intense, hard-fought.
A jumping joint
May disappoint
And bring a fouler food for thought.

The cheese ferments and casts a scent.
The mousey man,
    alas, poor gent –
The die was cast
To flabbergast,
And he must yet come up with rent.

One Grey at a Time

My mentor friend named Dori Anne,
Descended from a hearty clan.
Despite much wisdom to convey,
Her favorite sport is child's play.
Perhaps that's why she doesn't grey.

The silver lining of her years?
A couple strands behind her ears
Do glisten like a treasure fair --
Much like her heart, more than her hair.
Thus she has flair to share, I swear.

On the Bluff

A Hollywood agent was rough
Till one starlet called out his bluff.
She turned on her heel
To catch a new deal
And turned him to marshmallow fluff.

Ere long, she became a film star,
And bade him a big au revoir.
If wishes took wing,
His phone, it would ring.
But now he regrets from afar.

Out of Bounds

A woman who yearned for great fame
Refused to make honor her aim.
She reached for prime time,
On others to climb,
And so she was left with the blame.

'Tis true that success was a stretch,
Beyond what her talent might fetch.
Still, nose in the air,
In pride, unaware,
Superfluous speeches she'd sketch.

For monuments built out of place
Contribute, not fame, but disgrace.
And trophies to self
In dust on the shelf
Do little to help one save face.

Out of the Should-Work

"I could. I would. I should."
Such phrases knock us flat.
They're barely understood,
But worse than idle chat.

We ought for naught be caught
In traps these orders bait.
They only leave us fraught
With vows they obligate.

To should on self is rough.
To blame the past is vain.
Today is full enough
To weather and sustain.

Pachyderms at Play

Perky pachyderm

At play

Call to us;

    affirm

Hearsay.

Yell and stretch and squirm;

Daresay.

Every line

    long-term

Relay.

Mightiest may fall

Someday.

Anybody hears?

Take notes.

Pretty floppy ears

Lose quotes.

After years of tears,

Yield votes.

Party Line

There once was a government clerk,
Disgruntled with his type of work.
Then he had a fling
With sweet Silly String
And drove all his colleagues berserk.

He fiendishly sprayed out the twine,
As colleague did whimper and whine,
'Cept one friendly voice
Called out with a choice:
"Hey, get lost. But drop me a line."

Perturbia in Suburbia

While stepping out to grab the mail,
I caught some sights that made me wail.
And yet, I lived to tell the tale,
Although my home is now for sale.

My next-door neighbor, Mr. Schwartz,
Who works downtown in city courts
And congregates with high consorts,
Was on his porch in undershorts.

Across the street. Bud Overton
Played target practice with his gun.
He called his shots, "Four, three, two, one!"
And sent my puppy on the run.

Meanwhile, just three houses down,
The Tylers had stepped out of town.
A dozen teens looked like to drown
As kegs dispensed a liquid brown.

Then suddenly, a cry was heard,
But not from animal or bird.

It was a sound bizarre, absurd,
That came from old Miss Mallanerd.

A winged creature crossed the street.
It darted back and forth, offbeat,
And settled on her twill loveseat
Beneath her dainty stockinged feet.

"What's shakin', Mamma?" cried the fowl,
Just like a suitor on the prowl.
My spinster neighbor shook a towel.
Her Siamese began to growl.

The parrot flapped his wings and fled ;
He left his droppings on my head.
By now, bewildered, seeing red,
I chose to market my homestead.

I cannot sell the place too soon.
My neighborhood's a sick cartoon.
No longer my resort, cocoon.
And all this happened before noon.

Plea-Mail

Dear spammers and scammers, take heed.
Our mailboxes, they bulge indeed.
Your offers and spiels
And uncanny deals
Reveal never value, but greed.

The banks where we don't have accounts,
The freebies, all kinds and amounts –
Your most urgent pleas
Send us to our knees.
We beg you to desist and cease.

We're not gonna fall in your net.
In fact, we'd much rather forget.
We won't pay your bribe
Or things you describe.
So please unsubscribe us. You bet.

Pocketing the Difference

A worker was recently canned,
Departing without cash-in-hand –
Pursuing a dream,
Fell into a scheme,
Trespassing the law-of-the-land.

He heartily orders embraced
Till finally, embarrassed, disgraced,
He shouldered the rap
For Boss' big yap,
Developing worksite distaste.

But backfiring plots reward best.
Litigiously, he convalesced.
The gavel announced
And justice pronounced,
Refilling his empty war-chest.

Poetic License

Point no finger

Over wrong.

Ever linger –

Trusted song.

Intermingler,

Come along.

Look with leaning

Into themes.

Catch the meaning;

Eye the dreams,

Never keening

Sacred schemes.

Ever greening dawn the dreams.

Point Blank

To play strategic on the job,
Be careful whom you might hobnob.

A manager who works with me
Is bothered by not one,
    but three.
These cads will not give up the chase;
They constantly invade her space.

"Step back," she said,
    fair to exclaim.
The point is clear.
    It's not a game.
Your outcome's sure to disappoint;
Don't get your noses out of joint.

Look to yourselves,
    you garish guys.
Behind her head she might have eyes,
But never for the likes of you,
Because you do too hard pursue.

They disremember she's the boss,
Which leaves the rest of us at loss.
But soon they'll come up for review,
And they can bid a raise adieu.

Poker Face

There once was a woman named Ann,
So handsome they thought her a man.
She buried an ace
With her poker face
And took home the haul as she'd planned.

Ann had no dear dreams of delight,
Nor 'visioned herself clad in white.
She weathered the test,
Cards close to her chest,
And purchased her palace
    sans knight.

Poser

Without a murmur, if you please,
The artist's palette she'll appease.

To read the most creative mind,
The child may reflect mankind.

When by the shutter does she sit,
No vanity do we admit.

Will we regard, respect, or tease?
Or simply utter: "Sit. Say cheese"?

Puddle Power

Some see merely mud.
I behold a rainbowed whirl,
Iridescent glow.
PUDDLE POWER CALLS.
See the colors blend,
Ripping with the softest breath,
Not just oil spill.

Who needs rubber boots?
Grab your grubby sneakers fast.
Feel the soggy squish.
PUDDLE POWER CALLS.
Learn to walk again.
Feel the fun. The world is new.
Celebrate in style.

Pulling His Own Weight

A once famous player named Moe
Was sporting a new sort of glow.
He crowed at his wife
To blame for his strife,
Instead of the stuff he would stow.

His dental appointments raised dread,
And so did his middle-aged spread.
Guess that's the result
Of joining the cult
Of eating and drinking in bed.

Pulling Strings

A symphony cellist named Kate
Discovered her fate far too late.
A little off-key,
With no guarantee,
She never had time for a mate.

So Katie went tugging the string,
Despite her desire for a ring.
She kept perfect time,
Though missing her prime,
And only onstage did she swing.

Punched Out

Jean-Claude retired just last May.
He simply up and walked away.
The firm, he left in younger hands;
He'd had enough of its demands.

Ere long, his dance card he did fill
With new pursuits to fit the bill.
These days, he shops the internet
And daily parcels does he get.

In trendy togs, pristine and new,
He clicks the set, perchance to view –
One thousand shows to sample, swatch;
He says there's nothing on to watch.

He shops for munchies, treats and snacks
To eat his sweets and then relax.
We guess it stands as no surprise:
His other half does roll her eyes.

She's off to work or out to roam,
Because she's never home alone.

When she returns from toil and test,
He says, "Long day. I need a rest."

Perhaps he's earned this slower pace,
A chance to grab some breathing space.
Although she could retire in June,
She hopes to sing a different tune –

And maybe leave the house by noon.

Ragtop

She borrowed her best friend's ragtop one night,
Enjoying the great out of doors.
Arriving at last at a red traffic light,
She was met by four young troubadours.

These cocky young chaps began hooting in glee.
They tossed something into her car.
The light changed, one yelled,
 "Will you go out with me?"
Then they blasted off.
 "Gee, how bizarre."

She glanced in the back then,
 expecting the worst
From this wild bunch,
 who'd been quenching their thirst:
A raw egg, a dead mouse,
 or Heav'n only knows,
But all that she found
 was a single red rose.

"Still got it!" she said to herself,

and she steered,
With self-image soaring,
as they disappeared.
But she never drove topless again.
Who would dare?
'Cause not only flowers
may fly through the air!

Reading Between the Pines

I'm nestled in my nifty nook,
My fingers wrapped around a book.
Key characters draw me outdoor
To gather by the shady shore.

The plot has pleasant turns and twists.
The mystery proceeds, persists.
Its message true is evergreen,
Just like my secret woodsy scene.

Assignments call, but let me be.
Procrastination pardons me.
Another deadline's out of sight;
Perhaps I'll see to that tonight.

When pressure builds, constrains, confines –
Serenity's in storylines.
And here, where filtered daylight shines,
I've learned to read between the pines.

Restward Bound

I like to run in bright of day,
To see the sights and feel the fray.
It's still a mystery, a lark,
That steps are counted after dark.

When lo, my restless legs and heart
Accelerate more than their part.
Each morn, when all is done and said,
I've sprinted miles in my bed.

My coverlet's a twisted knot.
I've given everything I've got.
Without a foot upon the floor
I've run unmeasured miles or more.

The night-watch on my wrist is dark,
But still reports my parts don't park.
A marathon, put to the test.
It may be time to get some rest.

Rock On

Young Icarus carried a crush;
For Candy, his mind
    was a mush.
He failed at finesse,
His manners a mess –
Perhaps it was just a bum's rush.

He finally snagged up her soul.
They stepped out alone
    for a stroll.
She joined in his climb
For secrets sublime,
But more than their hearts were a-roll.

They roped both their girths to a rock,
But somehow declined
    to take stock.
The higher they scaled,
The more the rope failed.
The rest of the story's a shock.

Their ending, we fear, was profound.

Just ask anyone
    still around.
They vanished from sight,
Perhaps taking flight.
The secret remains underground.

Roll Tape with Mouths Agape

Unconscious and irrational,
Like toys we are played
And tossed into the bin
When the child loses interest.

Rag dolls and action figures,
We fall atop one another,
Waiting for attention.

Empty promises are
Senseless and absurd.
But we gobble them still,
Hoping this time
Our globe will spin
The other way.

"Roll tape!" we chant.
"Give us tales to tell
And stories to shout.
Tell us you really mean it this time.
Play us again."

But our batteries are losing juice.
We're becoming broken
With frayed edges
And faded faces.

Film at 11.

Rumormonger's Report

The shooter of scuttlebutt sits
And spins several yarns, as she knits.
She's flapping her jaw.
What's stuck in her craw,
While ripping an old friend to bits?

With chit-chat most vile and sham,
The gossip vends loud-spoken spam.
She'll tittle and tat,
A-chewing the fat,
With any old Miss or Madame.

Outside of her circle they fall,
Ripped out like torn rows in her shawl.
Unmended, they lie,
No chance to deny
The gall of her tales told so tall.

Shout and Spout

A man who was never in doubt
Opinions and orders did flout.
As parent, he'd prate,
But never would wait.
And soon, he'd abandoned his clout.

As each generation arose,
They shed him like yesterday's clothes.
He still would inflate
To pontificate,
Although no one pondered his prose.

Perhaps he had wisdom to share,
But others remained unaware,
Ignoring his bait
And tossed-around weight.
If only he'd come up for air.

Simply Driven

Resignation? No, not me!
It's something I could never be.
I'll struggle, scratch, cajole, and beg
To raise the bar another peg.
But signing off, I will not do.
I cannot lay it down. 'Tis true.

I'll labor till one day I'll fall,
Although my back's against the wall.
Determination sends me forth
To try to prove again my worth.
Of course I know it's in His hand;
It's idleness I cannot stand.

Resignation? No, not me.
It's something I could never be.

Sleepless CEO

Oh, my goodness! I'm the boss!
Will this quarter be a loss?
What about my angry board?
It's been months since I have snored.

Inventory's piled sky-high.
Orders dropped;
    I'm gonna fry.
Competition's got us beat.
Now I'm in the worry seat.

Offshore orders just fell flat.
Wait till Wall Street hears of that!
Our shares will drop,
    just like a rock,
And I'll be on the chopping block.

My shareholders are claiming fraud.
My secretary wants my bod.
My next-in-charge thinks he's my heir;
I caught him measuring my chair.

Two kids in college,
    needing cash.
The spouse just threw another bash.
The bills are coming;
    watch me duck.
The Rolls leaks oil,
    just my luck!

Insider trading?
    That's a laugh
The tax man wants my autograph.
They're pushing me
    right to the brink.
I might sleep better in the clink.

Snapshot

Snap a selfie.

Now you're trendy –

Apps attracting,

Posers plenty.

Show your best you.

Hold it steady.

Only friends view.

Truth: Shared. Ready?

Spam-Jam Flimflam

My most faithful pen-pal
　　by far,
This paperwork pirate bizarre
Does fill up my box
With unwelcome shocks,
If I leave my spam-guard ajar.

My gateway is framed
　　and secure,
And still I will hear from this boor –
With offers of prize
To lure, tantalize,
This cyberspace spam saboteur.

I'm putting a ban
　　on his bulk,
The letters from this ogre hulk.
He won't sign his name,
So I'm taking aim,
Reporting him, so he can sulk.

Henceforth, I'm committed

    to shred
His plentiful missives unread.
Won't open a note
Or card to promote
Whatever else from this bonehead.

Spring Break Mistake

A charm-worthy changeling
    might find this one cool,
Had she not contracted
    a germ at the pool.
Although there the spa was
    a-briny and hot,
The messy hotel just might warrant a shot.

Thus launched a vacation,
    as well as a lunch.
I'd offer more details,
    but you have a hunch.
It might have been magical,
    memories made,
Except that the lodging its beauty betrayed.

Alas to poor Erin,
    I must cheer my chime.
It's clear the spring hues
    are supreme and sublime,
But set by her countenance,
    matching a fern,

It's clear her condition is cause for concern.

At the risk of impugning
    a jubilant crew,
My musings hereto may soon
    set some askew.
Still, my singularity here
    may be seen,
Displayed in rhymed meter to underline green.

Stalk Options

A strapping youth we know as Jack
Did overreach beyond and back.
He scaled the heights, as we've been told
To find the goose with eggs of gold.

He stubbed a toe and scraped a knee,
Still upward scurried ceaselessly.
And though he came back empty-handed,
He could scarce be reprimanded.

The sights he saw would marvel most;
Young Jack was never one to boast.
His climbing days would last no longer,
Even though they made him stronger.

Lesson learned: Dream to the sky,
And ne'er forget 'tis false to fly.
A lofty treasure may appeal;
Returning home we find what's real.

Swearing Out His Welcome

There once was a fellow named Wayne,
Who spoke just in words most profane.
He'd drop the big bomb,
With motions aplomb,
And leave us with major migraine.

His small talk did burnish his shine,
As shelter we'd seek from malign.
The shadow he cast
Would leave us aghast
And cause us to make a beeline.

This clod, he would clatter and cuss,
And fume up his face in a fuss.
But never you mind,
For we're disinclined
To bid him with us to discuss.

Taking Umbrage

A puddle from poison pen beckoned.
A promise once broken was reckoned.
And under the laws,
The umbrella clause
Determined their fate in a second.

The cad claimed he felt much remorse.
The judge decreed no-fault divorce.
And that shady fella
Just like the umbrella --
His pre-nup held water, of course.

'Neath parasol sweet, she stepped out,
With nary a peep or a pout.
Her bell and her book
Both rang off the hook,
Once she was free-clear of that lout.

Tax Against the Wall

How can fiscals fly so fast?
Documenting, I'm aghast.
Confident? Put down that pen.
Push to shove? It's "when" again.
Help! By papers I'm harassed.

Tax prep time! I have to focus;
Need a little hocus-pocus.
Easy money? That's a joke.
Busted! Now I think I'm broke.
And my accountant's gonna choke.

Pounding buttons, hand to plow.
Look at me, subtracting now.
Number-crunching confidante?
Maybe I am part-savant.
Finished, but I don't know how.

The Tusker's Bluster

In hulk and bulk, he stands to strut
With tsk-tsk-tsk
    and tut-tut-tut.
His every step digs deeper rut.

Selective mem-ry guides his way.
He cherry picks to fill his fray,
Then bellows back,
    "It's me! Hooray!"

The gentle creatures step aside,
Their feathered faces thus to hide,
Lest they be baited to confide –

Until they understand the truth,
Long buried, ever since their youth.
A tusk falls short of wisdom's tooth.

Rise up, ye fearless fauna fair.
The looming lout had best beware.
Step up,
    and share your savoir-faire.

An elephant cannot forget?
It could be true somehow, but yet
We beg to differ,
    no regret.

For here's a secret, tough to keep,
Regardless if you look or leap.
The pachyderm is just skin deep.

Theory-Eyed

They're out to get us;

Have no doubt.

Eyes all around us

Ogling clout.

Round up the troops now;

Yield no ground.

Each low- and high-brow

Yells unsound.

Eschewing know-how

Deceit downed.

Thick and Thin

The elephant bull stomps and sweats.
He may give as good as he gets.
Still somehow we thunk
He might turn his trunk,
Escaping whatever upsets.

He'll pound the savanna to dust,
While grinding to grit any trust.
The beast bellows bold
To boast uncontrolled –
But never becomes upper-crust.

When wrinkles arise on his skin,
While energy runs ever thin,
He trumpets his call
And gives it his all
To chalk it all up as a win.

This Queue Shall Pass

Whoever said,
"Nothing lasts forever,"
Never caught the ladies' queue
At intermission
For a show like this.
"Standing-room only"
Takes on a whole new meaning
When the lights begin to flash,
And we're all still waiting
For thrones
Before we can return
To our seats.

Throwing to Extremes

When hobbies become habits
    and enjoyments grow extreme,
While pleasures turn to pesterings
    and joys aren't what they seem,
Addiction may take toxic turns
    and hold the captive fast.
And spices turn to poison,
    as the moments never last.

The highest of ambitions
    may be promptly overdone
To compromise convictions,
    burning bridges one by one.
An all-too healthy plan
    leaves moderation in its wake.
Exaggerated zeal may
    prove magnificent mistake.

Mere discipline can be enslaving,
    even soundest goals.
Though taken to extremes,
    they fill no holes deep in our souls.

As hedonistic, altruistic,
    unrealistic lines
May never lead to happiness;
    this routine joy declines.

Tight Spot

The trucker was proud of his place.
He put down his pager to race
Until a low ledge
Dismantled his edge –
Immediately he lost face.

Could be superstition at best.
Perhaps he just needed a rest.
Still, rules do not waive
For such a close shave,
So now he must retake his test.

Time Machine

Dear Tech Department, intervene!
I'd like to buy a time machine.
The hour has come;
    turn back the clock;
Don't tell me that you're out of stock.

Crank up those dials,
    make 'em spin,
And make my face turn young again.
Erase the wrinkles years have wrought
Without a single afterthought.

Cause all my locks to shine anew,
In my original hair hue.
Reverse ill gravity's effects,
And all my aging peers perplex.

Restore my balance, muscle tone,
But leave alone my funny bone.
I won't mind,
    if it hurts a bit,
To gain the youthful benefit.

Then switch to neutral,
    make it stop,
And I'll send others to your shop.
If you can make my life stand still,
My friends shall buy it too;
    they will!

Time Trials

My best friend's husband Nate
Is fearful to be late.
It's tick and tock
And run. Don't walk.
Just hurry up and wait.

His ever hurried state
Brings marital debate.
To live by clock,
No time to talk,
Affection does deflate.

The pace on her will grate.
This we anticipate.
We mean no knock,
But sense no shock,
At his turnover rate.

Trumpeting for Peanuts

The elephant never regrets.
He gives so much more than he gets.
He paves flat the way,
So others give sway,
Attempting to hedge all his bets.

He'll trumpet for peanuts. 'Tis fact.
And unload the pockets he's packed –
But only for show,
His boast to bestow,
And beg them to overreact.

He's never to be over-pomped,
At least by many he has stomped.
But everyone sees
The knock in his knees,
Despite his self-praise ever-prompt.

The world is a stage; so they say.
The elephant may lead the way.
At least for a time
And maybe a rhyme,

But truth will trump theater someday.

Savannas are samples to view
With creatures poor and well-to-do.
What lessons we learn
When bridges we burn,
And allies once pledged get their due.

Lo, now 'cross the plain sounds a strum –
No mirrored mirage, no humdrum.
The victory song
Will right every wrong
When King of Creation will come.

Can elephant never regret?
We ain't seen the last of it yet.

Unknown

Unbelievables

Never number

Knowledge's

Necessity.

Only the Omniscient's

Wonders will

Nudge Nature.

Vestiges of Voyages

I don't feel much like working here.
I'd rather be a buccaneer
And sail to sites still off the charts,
Adventuring in vacant parts.

I'd like to claim an honored quest,
With very valued goal obsessed.
Veracity is here required:
The husband recently retired.

My inspiration's growing thin
Amid the daunting daily din.
Here's my complaint and earnest plea:
"Turn down that mindless day TV!"

The furniture is rearranged,
And objects frequently are changed.
I cannot find my own supplies,
Which vanish right before my eyes.

Fresh recipes do scent the air.
New spices fill our kitchenware.

Strange objects now arise, appear:
New guest soaps, dishrags – there and here.

Forgive me, friend, for running on.
The pills may spill. We're overdrawn.
We've met a crossroads in our life.
I'm not sure now who is the wife.

So hoist the sails, mate. Sally forth!
Strap headphones on, for what they're worth.
I'm concentrating on my task.
And sipping from a dreamer's flask.

To self-employment still resigned,
This pirate cannot fall behind.
I'll hit the high seas in my mind.

Wake-Up Call

"Will you join me for hatha?"
    my fine friend tried.
"I drank one for breakfast,"
    I promptly replied.
"No, silly! It's yoga,"
    she eagerly said.
"They've already taught me
    to stand on my head."

We stretched into lycra
    and dashed to the gym
To learn six positions
    for stretching each limb.
My whole body ached,
    at the back of the room,
While the lady beside me
    full reeked of perfume.

The guru, he taught us
    to roll out our tongues
And pant like a dog
    at the top of our lungs.

AN ELEPHANT NEVER REGRETS

We postured and gestured
and reached way up high,
As he muttered mantras
to scents in the sky.

Before he dismissed us,
he stood straight and tall
And waved a bright crystal
out over us all.
Completely bewildered,
I packed up my tote
And slipped out the back
without rocking his boat.

My friend was delighted
I joined her that day.
She bade me become
her hatha protégé.
I gently refused,
as I started my car.
I wanted to answer,
"My dear, how bizarre!"

The next time the yoga class
arches and groans,
I'm heading directly

for coffee and scones,
Rebuilding my karma
    with stimulant sweet.
That certainly helps me
    get back on my feet.

I'm not slamming yoga,
    or I'd hold my peace.
For sure, it brings many
    both joy and release.
But plentiful protests
    from my creaky frame
Do dictate that I choose
    an alternate game.

Wary Warbler

A wary warbler, I've been known
To sing in solitude.
No, I'm not tone deaf. Hold the phone.
I don't mean to be rude.

It's just that I prefer to croon
Away from open ears.
I learn the lyrics, belt a tune –
No need for cheers or jeers.

My favorite solos I have sung
While piloting my car.
I've let 'er rip, busted a lung,
On road trips flung afar.

My music is a secret still.
Don't try to catch my song.
I'll chirp and chant and hum and trill
With none to sing along.

Watered-Down War

Zipping down the interstate,
Running late at half-past eight,
Children bickering in back –
Mother driver plans attack.
"Work it out," she says, irate.

Miles pass, as on they clash.
Backseat bounces, while they thrash.
She, white-knuckled, grabs a drink
Of her water, thus to think.
Then it hits her like a flash:
Ceasefire comes with one backsplash.

Don't look back to view the fray.
Creatively she'll yet convey –
Their signal swap,
Their faces sop,
Communicating with a spray.

Across one shoulder with one squeeze,
A full surprise from them she'll tease.
Thus startled, shocked,

Their battle blocked,
They'll settle in for moment's peace.

Ah, dear détente, they won't forget
The day their clothes were soaking wet.
How tiny tempers may improve,
If hydrated while on the move.
Teach lessons on the fly? You bet!

This mama, she won't text and steer,
But she can signal in high gear.
When kids may strive,
Still on she'll drive
But telegraph a message clear.

Waving Farewell

The season's final shot rang out,
Regatta to begin.
Our boat was strong;
    we knew the route,
Assured that we would win.

The fleet flew flags in every hue,
A seaborne rainbow scene.
Our spinnaker flapped red and blue,
But I was turning green.

The skipper held fast to the sheet;
He shouted out, "Jibe Ho!"
The boom spun 'round;
    I lost my feet
And felt my stomach blow.

I sprawled upon the starboard rail
And pitched over the side.
The first mate, he began to bail,
While looking on, tongue-tied.

The skipper tacked us back to shore,
Thus giving up our lead.
My shame complete forevermore,
The season to concede.

This sailor learned a lesson tough.
Of thus I have a hunch.
If we set sail when waves are rough,
I'd better hold my lunch!

Weep Show

When weeping won't wane,
And a whine turns to wail,
When pouring one's heart plain
Transforms to travail,

A strange sort of break may
Occur in the soul –
The floodgates of faith, they
Do one over-bowl.

Vast mountains of misery
Move just a wee smidge;
Forgiveness calms waters
Gone under the bridge.

'Tis then that one's weeping,
No mere sorrow show,
May move on to reaping
To best what we sow.

Whether Watch

My day was filled with glooms and dooms,
With clouded visage, poor presumes.
A closer look gave me a glance;
My days aren't dictated by chance.
No tempest or tornado looms.

The radar's not to be my trust.
Such worry's proved to be a bust.
Forecasts may fail,
While I travail.
Let faith be built on truth. It must.

So stir my heart. Begone, ye bug.
There's so much more than in my mug.
And que sera and lah-di-dah
Diminish not the bluest blah.
The answer's found in Heaven's hug.

Wicket Woman

A hard-working woman named Kay
Knocked off for a game of croquet –
She gave it a whack,
Discovered her knack –
Soon Kay was no work and all play.

Wonder in the Waiting

A marvel awaits,
     as we cease to attempt
To right every wrong
     and the Victor preempt.
We race far afield,
Forgetting to yield,
And cultivate strife.
     Thus, we harvest contempt.

We pique in a pickle
     and wrinkle fair brow.
We pause not for progress,
     our tempers endow.
And so in our prime,
We lost the sublime
To sacrifice joy
     on the altar of now.

The sudden has surely
     been much oversold.
Our striving earns nothing
     but shiny fool's gold.

Beginning again
In each now and then:
We might wonder what
    may our waiting behold.

Zillion Zigzags

Zipping and zooming,
Every signal sends us off,
Soul-borne GPS.

Who will call us home?
What magnetic pole directs,
If the arrow fails?

Footfalls may deceive,
A zillion zigzags mark time.
Destination waits.

About the Author

An award-winning poet and prolific writer, holding a B.A. in English and an M.S. in Journalism, Linda Ann Nickerson has worked as a professional writer for more than four decades.

She has also taught creative writing, poetry, and literature classes and has presented to adult writing workshops and groups.

In an earlier life, she worked as a book editor and widely-read reviewer of books on all types of topics.

Linda Ann writes news and feature columns for several well-known websites. Her published portfolio includes well over 5,000 web articles, as well as countless print pieces.

When she's not writing poetry, fiction, features, or promotional copy, Linda Ann may be found riding horses, running canine cross-country, biking trails, creating a quilt, or training for her next race. Or she may simply have her nose buried in another book, perhaps with a grandchild on her lap.

Other poetry books by Linda Ann Nickerson include:

- *ABCs of Acrostic Poetry: The Keyword is King*

- *Absent Nightmare Zinnias: Rhymed Acrostics from A to Z*

- *Fashion Victims: Missing Style by a Marvelous Mile*

- *Glass House Visions: Skipping Stones and Baring Bones*

- *Going Vertical: Acrostics in Action*

- *Horseplay Secrets: Learning in Rhyme from Equines Sublime*

- *Stealing Wonder: A Rhyming Race to Capture Grace*

- *What's in Santa's Sleigh This Christmas?*

www.ingramcontent.com/pod-product-compliance
Lightning Source LLC
Chambersburg PA
CBHW071428090426
42737CB00011B/1601